CW00394909

FROM A SPARK TO A FLAME

HOW TO BUILD A SUCCESSFUL MOBILE PIZZA BUSINESS

Jay Emery

FROM A SPARK TO A FLAME
Copyright © 2016 by Jay Emery
All rights reserved.

First published in 2016 by
Bushman Multi Media Publishing
20 Barnetts Close, Kidderminster DY10 3DG

This edition published in 2017 by
And Then Publishing

No part of this book may be used or reproduced in any
manner whatsoever without written permission except
in the case of brief quotations embodied in critical
articles or reviews.

For information contact
www.bushmanwoodfiredovens.co.uk

ISBN 978-0-9956955-8-0

DEDICATION
For my loving wife Elaine, fondly known and
forever referred to as the dragon.
Through all the ups and downs that life has
thrown at us, you have stood beside me,
believed in me and supported me, and for
that I am forever grateful.

CONTENTS

FOREWORD

I'm not exaggerating when I say that Jay Emery revolutionised the UK pizza industry.

His affordable, practical and sturdy wood-fired ovens were a game changer, but it was his approach to making pizza and making money that has become the standard at events, markets and (if you can get into the kitchen) restaurants up and down the country.

Within 20 minutes of meeting Jay, he had me making pizza, he made it easy and fun. His knowledge and enthusiasm but also his practical approach astounded me, as did the concept of wood-fired pizza ovens at outdoor events. His ovens were the first that could be transported from site to site without having to be built up (back breaking work) or cracking in transit, making authentic Neapolitan wood-fired pizza possible at events. It really was a game changer.

It was around this time that the first inklings of a street food scene were beginning to pop-up in pockets of London and it soon became apparent that Jay's ovens and systems for producing profitable pizza would be perfect for this fledgling industry. Before long, wood-fired pizza was at the vanguard of the street food revolution, with its laudable aim of democratising great food - making it both accessible and affordable.

When we first talked about street food, his eyes lit up "I've been doing that for years" he declared with a beaming smile. "But that's great, that it's taking off, how can I help" I could sense his brain moving at a thousand miles an hour, processing the possibilities, the opportunities.

When we set up Digbeth Dining Club back in August 2012 the only pizza man we called was Jay. We needed a professional to pull all of the other caterers along with him. These guys were green. They could cook but could they cook quick enough? Could they maintain a consistently high quality? Could they keep their spirits up when it rained or even on occasions snowed? Would they give up if they lost money?

He didn't let us down. When I look back now I realise what a mentor he was to the newbies and what a rock he was for our fledgling event. Jay was a key member of the Digbeth Dining Club family and one of the UK's first wood-fired pizza / street food businesses — almost certainly the first profitable one.

One of my favourite memories of the time was when Jay turned up without any staff for a particularly busy gig. He saw the fear in my eyes. "It's fine, I'm doing an honesty box" he laughed back at me. An honesty box, in a dark carpark in inner city Birmingham?! But that's what we love about him. He's always coming up with new ideas, new ways of working, taking risks while smiling and laughing and shouting banter at his fellow traders and customers.

Whenever I speak to a start-up looking to do pizza the first thing I ask is 'have you met Jay yet?' and then I give them his number if they haven't. The support he provides has helped to develop long lasting and profitable businesses, probably several hundred in the past few years.

Reading this book will give you a true insight into how to set up and run a successful wood-fired pizza business. In the next few years I expect that this book will be seen as the manual, or even the bible for wood-fired pizza businesses.

It's not easy running your own food business and those that try to do it on their own, often fail. This book should be your companion throughout the planning, developing, launching and running stages of your new business – don't be without it!

Mark Laurie
Director of the Nationwide Caterers Association & Streetfood.org.uk

INTRODUCTION

Welcome to the wonderful world of wood-fired catering!

If you're reading this, you've probably seen pizza vans serving delicious pizza at festivals or farmers markets and thought I wonder if I could do that? Well, if you're serious about starting a mobile wood-fired oven business or curious about what you might need to get started then you've come to the right place.

Since 2010 I have helped more people start mobile pizza businesses than anyone else. I have customers who have turned over thousands of pounds in their first year to companies that are turning over £250,000 in year three. What's more, I have over 80% success rate for new business start-ups, which blows normal start-up statistics out of the water.

So what does it take to be successful? Sometimes I wish it were as simple as just building an oven, chucking it on a trailer or in a van and taking it round the country. Back in 1999 that's how I started. But I've paid my dues, perfected my ovens, worked out all the short cuts and now I'm in a position to help you. Like in any business, having insider information is the short cut to being successful and that's where I come in. But I also have to be honest with you. Not everyone can afford my help or my ovens. That's why I wrote this book.

If you were in my showroom, I would ask you all sorts of questions about your goals and dreams to work out the best option for you and how to make it happen. But for now, while you're reading this book, I'll walk you through the different options, let you know what works best for what type of business and give you all the questions you need to ask yourself. I'll also talk you through some of the nuts and bolts of running a mobile pizza business – including some of those lessons I learnt the hard way.

Obviously, if you're serious about building a wood-fired pizza business I want you to come and talk to me and buy one of my ovens (they are the best!) but if you're just putting your first toes in the water then this book will get you started and help you think through the things you'll need to work out.

And of course, there is nothing stopping you from using a competitor's oven or trying to work it all out yourself. But you'll find it a harder road to take, fraught with many obstacles. Setting up a new business is hard enough. If you're setting up a mobile pizza business, then choosing a Bushman wood-fired oven just makes life easier – just take a look at some of my customers' success stories.

I hope you enjoy reading this book and it gets your creative and entrepreneurial juices going. If you'd like to take things further, the next step is to attend one of my two-hour discovery sessions in Kidderminster. You will learn more about selling pizza than you could experience in six months on your own. And by the end of the session you will know without doubt if this is the right path for you.

But if you can't wait until then to find out what it's like to run a mobile pizza business on a day-to-day basis, go to www.bushmanwoodfiredovens.co.uk/dayinthelife and sign up to receive "A day in the life of a wedding caterer" – a free, 11-page blow-by-blow account of how to deliver exceptional service and make the maximum profit when catering with pizza at a wedding.

I really hope that we get to meet. My contact information can be found at the end of the book.

Happy Reading!

Jay Emery
Master Oven Builder & CEO
Bushman Wood-Fired Ovens

SO WHY WOOD-FIRED PIZZA THE BUSHMAN WAY?

No doubt you will have seen the increasing number of street food vendors in the UK. Even the food at your average music festival is better than it was 5 years ago. These traders must be onto something, right? But what most people don't know is that street trading is not the only game. It's just the entry point to the much more lucrative and easy to manage private catering market. And what's more you don't need to have any specific skills to succeed, just a strong desire to do well and the energy and ability to work for yourself.

Since 1999 I have been cooking food in wood-fired ovens. I'm originally from South Africa and I just love a good braai (OK that's a BBQ to most of you). Nothing beats cooking with fire.

When I came to the UK I was excited about bringing good BBQ to Brits. But in exploring the catering model and especially the street food model I could not find a way to really do BBQ without potentially incurring huge losses. The cost of ingredients was so high and there was a lot of wastage.

What I did find was a model with a guaranteed market approval and that had as close to zero wastage as you can get. It has a high-perceived skill requirement and simply outrageous gross profit margins: wood-fired pizza.

When I started doing wood-fired pizza catering it was a new market. Since 2010 there has been a mini explosion of street food traders but within this only a relatively small number of mobile pizza vendors.

That's not because the model is not good, it's because there's a barrier to entry that not all can afford. So depending on what kind of pizza selling model you are looking to set up, you are going to need at least £15,000 to get your business up and running at entry level. Depending on the model and your vehicle, this can rise to as much as £64,000. Not all that money is for the oven but it's fair to say that one of my wood-fired ovens is going to set you back at least £6,500. That's a lot more than a grill or a crêpe or coffee machine. But remember, a low barrier to entry often leads to market saturation.

While this book is primarily about mobile pizza catering, it's fair to say that I've helped quite a few newbies start up restaurants as well. But to be honest while I know I've got guts, I think people who start up a restaurant are the bravest of the brave. I'm not saying that it's not the right thing to do, but boy have you got your work cut out for you. Yes, the mobile model is more complicated but the restaurant model is more uncertain. You commit to a location and its associated demographic from the start (you can't just start the engine and move on if you've picked the wrong spot). Even when you have all that nailed down, you then have all the local taxes and rates, water and electrics and staff to contend with.

With a mobile business you can take the business to the people and you only need to employ staff when you need them (if you need them at all). Your biggest expense is going to be your mobile catering unit and that's a lot less than the rent you are going to have to pay someone else. And you'll own your catering unit. You can open for trade when you want and close when you want. If you do find that sweet spot of location/demographic *then* you could open your own restaurant – you'll have a head start knowing who your customers are and how many of them are out there.

The only down side of the mobile business I can see is the weak trade in January and February but plenty of my customers turn that to their advantage. They close up and go traveling, doing all the things that they would never be able to do if they had a restaurant.

The mobile model I describe in this book is as easy as pie to manage and operate with minimal equipment, minimum staff and completely flexible working hours. Plus you can make between 75-93% gross margin. There is certainly big money to be made if you want it.

My most dedicated and hardworking caterers are turning in excess of £350,000 a year all from a couple of vans. Other customers choose to use the model to generate a holiday fund, working occasional evenings and weekends only. This is no get rich quick scheme but you can find the lifestyle you want if you follow the model and run with it.

So if you do have the budget, and pizza appeals, here's why the Bushman pizza model is a great one to consider:

Great profit margins

If you're considering mobile catering as a business, then pizza makes a great choice.

The waste is minimal and the profit margins are great. A pizza cooked in 45 seconds from fresh has an average sale value of between £6 and £12 and a gross margin of around 90%. (If you'd like a closer look at how I make money catering for private events, sign up for my free detailed 11-page report "A Day in the Life of a Wedding Caterer" at www.bushmanwoodfiredovens.co.uk/dayinthelife.)

Flexibility

There are no guarantees in life but if you work hard and implement my model (you have access to a detailed operations manual when you buy one of my ovens), you can really create a great flexible lifestyle, selling pizza from a mobile wood-fired oven.

Some of my customers ease themselves into the business doing weekend gigs while holding down a full time job, others jump right in. It doesn't matter what you did in a former life, if you like people, aren't afraid of hard work, are good at following systems and procedures (or able to employ people who are) then this is a great business opportunity. Some of my customers include former building surveyors, accountants, catering college students and sourdough enthusiasts.

And don't forget a wood-fired oven isn't just for pizza – you can do pulled pork baps etc.

A premium product

Pizza is safe. Everyone has their favourite pizza. Grannies love them. Kids love them. There's no risk in buying a pizza. And the fact that most people don't have a wood-fired oven at home makes the pizza they buy from you extra special and able to bear a premium price.

Let's put that into perspective. We sell a Margarita pizza for £6 irrespective of what the burger bloke next to us charges because good pizza cooked in a wood-fired oven is perceived to be a premium product. Yet it costs us just 40p in ingredients. That's a whopping £5.60 profit every 45 seconds. With the overheads of just a two man team. Or an equivalent profit of £2.80 per person.

Cooking in a wood-fired oven looks hard (and impressive) but it's just a matter of practice. If you can cook a pancake you can cook a pizza. And if you can't do that then don't worry because I can teach you.

Loads of support and all the short cuts

Experience doesn't come cheap and when you buy one of my ovens I have a complete operations manual with all the advice, tricks and techniques you need to be successful. From dough ball management to tendering tricks to marketing to growing your business. When you do your research you'll see that there are cheaper ovens out there. But they are not as efficient or reliable and they don't come with access to my knowledge and experience. That's priceless. An expensive oven costs less than a cheap oven when the information and support you get with it saves you money and increases proficiency and productivity in the long run.

To give you an example, I was at a food festival recently in Birmingham. There were six pizza vendors in total and a couple of drinks vendors.

Three of the pizza vendors were customers of mine, two trading from stand in vans and one from a no frills trailer. They were all heaving, churning out a steady flow of pizza all at premium prices. They had the model and the sequence that I had taught them nailed down. One van was a one-man band, the other stand in van had three staff and there were two people working the no frills trailer. The average offering was £10 and each one finished the gig having sold about 200-250 pizzas.

In contrast the other three caterers had real problems.

One of the caterers had all the gear but no idea. He had an absolutely huge oven that could have held 8–12 pizzas at a time but because it was so big he could not get it up to temperature fast enough and ended up cooking one pizza at a time. Even then it took 5 min to cook each one – max capacity 20 per hour but potential customers just walked away when they saw how long it took to cook.

A second caterer specialised in desert pizza which is a great idea but she had 5 people working her stand when 2 would have done and undervalued her offering, selling at £3–£4.50. Her oven was not brilliant with no thermal mass so every pizza was over or under cooked. I would be very surprised if she made profits of more than £100.

The last vendor started on a shoe string. They had two cheap ovens each capable of cooking one pizza at a time. But having two ovens does not speed things up when they are low mass ovens since you now have two fires to manage and make all the pizza.

Again, I don't think I ever saw more than two people waiting for a pizza. Their wait was then made longer when one of the chefs in his wisdom thought that by closing the oven door he would be able to cook faster. Oops! This just put out the fire and made a smoky mess!

Had any one of them invested in one of my ovens and my systems, the profits they would have made in just a couple of days would have more than made up for the extra expense.

Making pizza the Bushman way is easy

Despite what the Italians would have you think, making great tasting pizza is easy if you follow my simple steps. You don't need to be a skilled pizziolo with years of experience to cook great pizza. When I've taught you how to make a good pizza you won't believe how easy it is. 120 customers cooking over 1.8 million pizzas a year in my ovens can't be wrong.

As I always say, if you can cook a pancake, you can make a pizza.

bushman wood fired ovens

THE FIVE MOBILE BUSINESS MODELS - CREATING A CATERING UNIT THAT WORKS FOR YOU

Trailer or vehicle? Which is right for your business plan?

In my opinion there are five different ways or models you can use to "deliver" pizza to a customer. Basically you have a choice between using a trailer or a converted vehicle to transport your oven. Your van could be a classic vehicle or modern. Your trailer could be no-frills or high end. Each model has a different entry level cost but those costs can rise depending on the extras you want to put in. Before you set your heart on a classic van conversion (costing tens of thousands of pounds), do consider the fact that each of these five models has basically the same earning potential.

Should you house your oven in a trailer or a vehicle? There is no one size fits all solution. Each option has its own merits and downsides. Basically, the right unit for you will depend upon what sort of business you're looking to create. Each of the models attracts a different ideal customer base so your business plan should really inform your choice.

1 Stand-in trailers

The stand-in trailer is exactly as it sounds. It's a trailer that you can actually stand in e.g. a horsebox, burger van style or specially built unit.

A stand-in trailer works perfectly in lots of settings. You've got room to work, plenty of space to keep everything you need and a great weatherproof environment around you.

Because of their size stand-in trailers are best suited to open space functions (e.g. festivals) or permanent/semi-permanent pitches (e.g. garden centres). Access restrictions usually mean they aren't suitable for the domestic party market, which is a lucrative area, so consider this before you choose a catering unit. You will also need to make sure the trailer is stored at a secure location. You'll also need a Land Rover or similarly powered vehicle to transport the trailer (and may need to install a tachograph which will limit the hours you can drive and your speed.)

2 Converted vehicles

an H-van

Modern vans are by far the most popular choice, closely followed by those who opt for an H-van. But there are a huge number of things that you need to consider before you choose one or the other – cost being the main one. I remember back in 2010 when cost about £4,000 now you are lucky to get one for £22,000. At Bushman Wood-Fired Ovens, we have helped people with conversions of VW Crafters, Renault Traffic Vans, Mercedes Sprinters and Citroen H-Vans to name but a few.

A converted vehicle can be a great way to go but it can be a pricey option as even after the initial purchase you have to convert and maintain them.

Should I buy second hand or new?

If you are going to purchase a second hand vehicle, I urge you to consider an approved dealer. Second hand vehicles can have low mileage and are a fraction of the price of a new one. Some reputable second hand dealerships will even offer finance and more importantly they often offer the option to purchase extended warranty.

There are 0% finance offers available on new vehicles, so this may be a better option than getting a second hand vehicle. My second hand vehicle has just cost me £3,000 to keep on the road, yet monthly repayments to own a new vehicle are just £269 per month....

When checking out the vehicle make sure it is long enough. I think an internal length of 4 metres is about perfect. I have known caterers who have fitted their unit into 3.5m but it's really tight. Longer than 4 metres is somewhat excessive in my opinion.

Another factor which you should consider is the height of the vehicle, a high top is better and ventilation in the roof is always good as it lets some of the hot air out.

If you are buying a new vehicle I would suggest that you register it before you have it converted. I have had a couple of customers who haven't done this because they wanted the maximum warranty. It led to huge complications at the DVLA because they had to declare the conversion which then needed to go through type approval. This may not be a major issue for you but it will cost you money and time – two things you don't want to waste.

Quirky. Beware of quirky. I've spoken to loads of people who wanted to do quirky. I've even not sold ovens to people who wanted to do them quirky. They've gone on to buy from another supplier but four years later they still don't have a viable business. I have a strictly no BS policy. If what you suggest is a fantastic idea, I'll tell you. But if it's not, I'll tell you anyway. In this business you need to be big enough to take the criticism. My customers are successful because they are not shrinking wallflowers. So if you can take the criticism and are prepared to learn then I'm here to help you.

Something else to consider with a vehicle conversion is that space can be tight so you will almost always need an additional back up vehicle or trailer with refrigeration for longer (2–3 day) functions.

If you're doing a long event, you might need to get off site to buy more supplies or drive to your overnight accommodation. In this case, you will need another vehicle, because most event organisers don't like vehicles to leave pitches before the end of the event.

It's true that a classic vehicle conversion gives you a fantastic USP (unique selling point) and some serious street credibility but they can be temperamental, so if you intend to do heavy mileage, think carefully as you may be better off with a trailer or a new vehicle.

If you opt for a vintage vehicle it is important to keep it running in tip top shape, so when budgeting take into account mechanics fees and vehicle upkeep and breakdown cover. You'll probably also need to convert the engine to comply with low emission regulations and this could cost you a fortune (especially in London). There are exceptions to really old vehicles but check it out. It costs me a fortune every time I want to drive to London with my pickup and people with Land Rovers have the same problem, so check it out before committing to spending loads of money.

Inevitably, as with most vehicles, breakdowns will happen. Breakdown cover will cost you money but missing an event due to vehicle problems could cost you your reputation. Please take all this into account and choose your vehicle and insurance carefully.

3 Stand-outside vehicles

There is also the stand outside vehicle model which is perfect for a small business.

We have helped several people convert Piaggio Apes, Tuc Tucs and Piaggio Porters.

These vehicles are small – tiny in fact – but we have worked out a way to fit the perfect compact and complete kitchen including oven, which means they are good enough for street trading, fantastic for small festivals and ideal for private parties.

You don't need to invest in a tow vehicle and it really packs a visual punch. The only downside is the cost of the vehicle and coachbuilding.

4 Stand-outside trailers

I love the stand-outside trailer model. Of all the mobile options it's my personal favourite. There are no speed limitations or restrictions for driving on the motorway. And if you think we've compromised on functionality, think again. We've managed to fit the most amazing compact kitchen into a trailer.

The different oven options offer lots of flexibility but a stand out trailer is still not for everyone. For one thing you'll need extra gazebos and it may not draw the crowds in the same way a van conversion can.

A stand-outside trailer is compact, lightweight and very functional. They're fantastic for almost any situation. Almost … if the weather's bad, you have a problem. But then irrespective of the unit, if the weather is bad, you won't have customers. Bad weather is the only nemesis in this business.

Stand-out trailers also present you with a refrigeration challenge, which can be expensive to get round especially if a custom-built solution is required. Some incorporate refrigeration into their towing vehicle. This may solve the problem and keep costs down too.

Benefits of a stand-outside trailer include:

- You deal with your customer at eye level, which allows you to build rapport

- It takes up a tiny amount of storage space

- It works fantastically for any private party or 1 to 3 day event

- You can use a relatively small van for towing, giving you value for money and space for other gear

- It will fit into most gardens so you can service private parties with ease

You're still going to need between twenty and twenty-five thousand pounds to get your business up and running. Not all of that goes on the oven and trailer – you'll also need gazeboes, generators and tools of the trade and that's where so many people go badly wrong. Trying to do this on the cheap just doesn't work.

5 No-frills stand-outside trailer

The no-frills trailer is our entry level catering solution. It's basically an oven on a trailer. But what an oven, and what a trailer! Whichever Bushman oven you choose it will be able to cook delicious thin based pizza in 45 seconds. A two man team can churn out 70 pizzas an hour using the medium oven. With the no-frills stand outside trailer, that's a lot of customers served quickly with the least possible overhead. And long experience has taught us that farmers' trailers are the best. They may not look pretty but they don't rust and given the vagaries of British weather this is crucial. And who wants to take half an hour to polish the mud off a pretty, shiny trailer every time they set up?

As with the previous model you'll also need preparation tables, washing facilities, cooler box storage and suitable awning coverage. By suitable, I mean an awning or gazebo that is weather proof and that doesn't blow away or collapse in high winds. Not a cheapy from Argos.

The big plus with our no frills trailer is that it will fit in to most single garages so it's easily kept at home. No storage costs for you!

A final note

Rear mounting an oven is a mistake made by people who don't know better.

On the internet I have seen some basic trailers with the oven mounted facing backwards, but I am telling you that your oven should face to the side. Why? Well, I too used to mount my ovens facing the back.

I soon learnt that this was a bad idea, especially if you are planning to do street trading or market pitches. Standard market pitches are 3m by 3m so if the oven is end mounted you will need a double pitch – since the trailer is 3m long you will need another pitch to serve in, costing you more. Mounting your oven at the back of your trailer will also pose a problem if you work in private gardens where space is limited.

That being said, sometimes there are occasions when being able to work off the back of a trailer is good. So really the answer to all of your problems is a rotating oven like this one mounted on our no-frills trailer.

Selecting a Coachbuilder

I've helped a lot of people get into the mobile catering business and one thing I've learned is that some coachbuilders promise the world and deliver the bare minimum. And if you don't go for our no-frills trailer but want to convert a vehicle or stand in trailer then you're going to need a coachbuilder.

I've seen some fantastic work, and equally I've seen some jobs that a person with basic carpentry skills could have done much better.

In short some coachbuilders are good and some are not.

And most of them seem to recommend something that's easy (for them) to build but that turns out to be hard (for you) to operate as a catering unit.

Fair enough; they're coachbuilders, not caterers. But there have been so many occasions when my proposed layouts have been altered during the build, leaving the caterer suffering with poor workflow and slow service when operating. Even a door that opens the wrong way will create havoc!

Making and selling pizzas ... I've been there and done it. The coachbuilder hasn't.

Make sure you think about how your unit will operate! Planning is critical – get it wrong and it could spell disaster.

At the very least, you'll have two people working in or outside your unit. They both need a designated place to perform their functions. One of them will be making the pizzas and putting them in the oven. The other will be taking orders and payments, cutting pizzas and serving drinks (if applicable). All operators need access to all their gear without having to cross each other or get each other to move out of the way.

This means for example that:

1. The workflow should be dough roller to preparation area to oven. Then on the other side from oven to counter to till

2. Dough balls should be with the dough roller

3. Gastro trays should be at working height, so you can grab your toppings and throw them on your bases

4. The order rack should be positioned near the till

5. Everybody needs to be able to get to the hand washbasin easily.

We're happy to help you

Fitting all this into a vehicle or trailer and arranging it can be a daunting task.

At Bushman Wood-fired Ovens we know that many of our customers are new to mobile catering or self-employment. That's why we are happy to hold your hand through the process of setting up your business. If you've decided this lifestyle is right for you and chosen your oven, the next most important step is to choose a good coachbuilder and design your layout. So, once you've paid your deposit on your oven we are with you every step of the way.

I offer all this help simply because I want you to be so successful that you come back for a second, third and fourth oven! I don't make any money from the sale or conversion of vehicles; I'm an oven man. I'll only sell more ovens if people make good decisions with their units and their business is growing.

If you decide not to buy one of my ovens, please, please pick a builder who has experience building mobile pizza units and get references! There's a lot to consider and plenty of scope to get it wrong. I've even seen people who should have known better, mess it up on their second and third units.

For now, I'll give you just one of my coach building horror stories to illustrate my point. On one job gastronorm tray slots had been cut in to a sheet of plywood covered in plastic. The ply wasn't edged, resulting in a cut and bacteria hazard. Apparently edging was part of the "extras" and would cost more. As you can see, you really do need to speak to someone who's done a lot of pizza conversions, not just one or two.

Driving with your trailer

Going for a trailer? It's critical to choose the right towing vehicle. Here's a summary of the key areas to think about when towing a trailer.

Will you need a tachograph?

This records the hours you drive and there are limits that you can't legally breach.

If the combined maximum plated weight of the trailer and tow vehicle exceeds 3.5 tonnes and you will be more than 70 miles from the base, you'll need a tachograph in your tow vehicle.

The DVLA don't like giving written explanations of how this works. So here's my best answer after paying more fines than I'd care to admit. If the gross total plated weight of a vehicle plus gross plated weight of the trailer is more than 3.5 tonnes and you will be more than 70 miles from your home you will need a tacho or you will be fined £300 per offence, non-endorsable. This all has to do with towing for reward and someone other than the vehicle owner driving the towing vehicle, distances to be travelled and so on. It sounds confusing so do give them a ring.

Will you need an operator's license?

If the unladen weight of the trailer is over 1,050kg, you may need an operator's license. That's the weight of just the trailer before it's fitted out. If you're not sure, again I urge you to contact DVLA for more information. Please note that some horseboxes can fall into this category. A horsebox is only exempt if it's for your own personal enjoyment (i.e. horse riding is your hobby) but for use in a business it is not.

My vehicle recommendation

I recommend that your vehicle has a minimum towing capability of 1.5 tonnes and a ball hitch capacity of 200kg (don't go for the standard 70-120kg). I've got a big 4 x 4 Nissan Navara, but it can only carry 120kg on the ball and my unladen trailer weighs 140kg on its hitch which means I have to do some jiggery pokery with ballast to get the trailer balanced.

Check also that your vehicle's tow ball is the same height as your trailer (normally 450mm) otherwise you're in for some costly conversion work! Basically, don't risk being overweight on your trailer or hitch point; both can lead to expensive disasters.

Trailer Towing License Conditions

Driving with a Trailer? There are License Conditions that you will need to meet.

If you got your driving license before 1 January 1997, you can tow trailers without any further testing, as long as the vehicle and trailer combination adds up to no more than 8.25 tonnes. You can also get provisional entitlement to drive a heavier combination; contact DVLA for details.

Assuming all other legal requirements are met, a braked trailer should not weigh more than the manufacturer's towing limit for the tow car. The towing vehicle's maximum gross train weight should also not be exceeded. (Train weight is the combined weight of the towing vehicle and the trailer.)

Unbraked trailers cannot weigh more than 750kg and the towing vehicle must have a kerb weight of at least twice the maximum weight of the trailer unless specified otherwise in the operations manual.

For towing vehicles with a maximum laden weight of under 3,500kg, the maximum trailer dimensions are 2.3m wide and 7m long (excluding the tow coupling and drawbar). This information applies to towing vehicles and trailers with a maximum laden weight of less than 3,500kg. Above this is HGV territory and totally different rules apply and boy you don't want to go there!

Car drivers who passed their driving test after 1st January 1997 are subject to greater restrictions on towing. You can tow a vehicle and trailer combination weighing up to 3.5 tonnes, provided that the unladen weight of the towing vehicle is greater than the maximum permissible weight of the trailer.

You can also tow a trailer with a gross weight of 750kg behind any category B vehicle - giving a maximum permissible weight of 4.25 tonnes (max weight for category B is 3.5 tonnes).

In practice, these new rules are not too restrictive for most drivers, but there are a few surprising exceptions. For example, large 4x4 pickups (like the Nissan Navara and Toyota Hilux) often have gross weights over 2.5 tonnes. This means that when coupled with a medium-sized caravan or other trailer (weighing >1 tonne), the combined gross weight would be likely to exceed 3.5 tonnes, which would be illegal.

If you want to tow greater weights and you passed your test after 1st January 1997, you'll need to take a further test. Contact DVLA for details. To find out the unladen weight of your towing vehicle, look in the owners' manual.

To find out the maximum permissible weight of a trailer, look for its 'plate' — a metal plate somewhere on the trailer that will state the maximum laden weight of the trailer.

One more thing — buy a locking wheel clamp and use it!

Note DVLA change the rules regularly, so not even the Enforcement Officers are up to speed so make sure you know what you can and can't do and always know what your loaded weight is. Remember the rule applies whether you are driving loaded or unloaded as I found out to my cost. It's the maximum permissible weights not the minimum weights that's important.

CHOOSING YOUR OVEN THE BUSHMAN WAY

The most important part of your set up is your oven. It's the engine that supplies the pizza and it's critical to get it right.

What you want versus what you need

Buying an oven involves investing a substantial amount of money into one product, so you have to be sure that you're getting exactly what you need and nothing more.

I've watched sales people getting customers to choose ovens that are way too large for their needs.

Why? Because that's selling: find out what the punter wants and sell it to them.

But there's an important difference between what you think you want and what you actually need. With ovens, size really isn't everything!

I once heard a salesman telling a customer that his oven was the best choice because it could cook eight pizzas at a time, compared to the competitor's, which only had space for three.

That sounds logical until you realise that the oven was to be fitted in a van that only had room for two people – three at a push. There's no way such a small van team could prepare anywhere near enough pizzas to keep such a huge oven at capacity. Not to mention the amount of wood it would take to keep it at optimum temperature and the extra weight in a van. Big problem!

At a recent food festival I attended this was also the case. I saw a couple with a huge oven. It took four hours to get the oven hot but they could only cook one pizza at a time due to the lack of skill and the wrong equipment. While another had two ovens each taking four minutes to cook one pizza. So slow. Remember the earlier story of the pizza festival – all the gear and no idea? It's a classic example. So pick the right sized oven for the job and consider where the oven is going to do its work.

My approach is totally different. I want my customers to be profitable as quickly as possible, so I save them money and heartache by selling them an oven that meets their needs. When things take off, I know they'll come back to me to buy another one!

I also know my ovens inside out. I have spent years researching and developing clay oven making techniques. I'm in the factory every afternoon building ovens. I use my ovens when I cater at private functions. I've cooked and sold pizza at festivals, farmers markets, charity events – you name it, I've done it. Not many sales people can say that.

In fact, most of my competitors don't have a clue how to run a pizza business, never mind use the oven for cooking – try asking them about dough ball management and see what happens! They will probably give you a recipe!!

So if you decide not to buy a Bushman oven, make sure that you're talking to someone who knows the mobile pizza business, knows about ovens and actually considers what you need rather than what they think they could get away with selling you. There is now so much choice on eBay, how are you supposed to know? Easy. If it's cheap, it's cheap for a reason.

The Bushman Oven range

Bushman Ovens come in small, medium, large and extra-large sizes. Each Bushman Oven is handmade to order and built to a client's exact specifications based on how and where they intend to use the oven.

Our medium oven is the most popular option for mobile caterers. It's capable of cooking 300 pizzas a day or 70 pizzas an hour with a two-man team.

If built into one of our no-frills trailers, the unit is low enough to be locked away overnight in a standard garage but high enough so that you don't break your back cooking pizza. But just because it's our entry level set up don't assume it's inferior in any way. It's got everything you need to make a hugely successful business.

You'll also want to consider the extras when budgeting/planning your business.

We also offer an onion shaped oven. There's no difference in the cooking ability but the shape is beautiful and makes an impressive statement at any event. The onion shape does make for a higher oven so getting into a standard garage can be tricky. If access is a must, then the low onion profile oven is a definite alternative.

If you're on a trailer and have the budget, then upgrading to a 360° rotating oven is a no brainer. Now you will be able to use your oven from any side of the trailer. This is invaluable if a pitch is small or tricky to access.

Oven thermometers

When you first start to cook pizza you'll want accurate temperature readings so that you know you are doing the right thing.

Most people assume that you can use a regular baking thermometer in your wood-fired oven and to a certain extent this is true, however you cannot put the thermometer into the oven during firing, because the extremely high temperatures reached by a wood-fired oven would destroy a standard oven thermometer.

The soot will also blacken the thermometer making it unreadable in some cases. And although standard oven thermometers are relatively inexpensive, unfortunately they can't give you residual heat readings and are only accurate at the instant the oven door is opened. Plus you can't read the temperature whilst the door is closed, so the readings may be inaccurate.

Laser thermometers have proved a popular choice for many but if you opt for a laser model make sure you purchase one that reads temperatures up to at least 550°C. Most standard laser thermometers will only read up to 300°C and they are useless when it comes to measuring heat in a wood-fired pizza oven, since the temperature you need to cook your pizza will be a least 350°C.

They are also problematical because they can only record a surface temperature, so for example, you could record a floor temp of over 350°C just 15 minutes after you have lit the fire, but the heat will not have penetrated deep enough at this point.

At Bushman, our solution is to offer built in temperature probes and thermometers which can track all the data you need:

- A thermometer to read the air temperature whether the door is open or closed

- A probe to record the real floor temperature

- A stored energy probe on top of the dome underneath the insulation - so you know how much heat you have or don't have

Why do we offer all these options?

If you use your oven to cook bread or meat you'll need to know the air temperature.

When cooking pizza you need to know that the floor temperature is at least 350°C in order to cook your pizzas to perfection in under 90 seconds.

The stored energy probe lets you know how long you can cook for without adding any more fuel.

Whilst thermometers may be important for the beginner, it is really practice and experience that will give you all the knowledge you need to cook the perfect pizza. However, knowing your oven is perfectly balanced and absolutely accurate when all 3 probes read the same, will give you complete peace of mind and enable you to cook absolutely any recipe from any cookbook.

An air probe can be retro fitted at any time by drilling a hole through the wall of the oven and putting a thin probe down into the oven. The under floor and dome probes cannot be retro fitted and need to be installed at the time of manufacture.

You could opt for three probes and one thermometer then simply plug the thermometer into whichever probe you want to use.

THE 5 GOLDEN RULES OF THE PIZZA BUSINESS

Like all rules there's a lot of learning (i.e. mistakes I've made) that has gone into their making. And there's a lot more detail that sits behind them as well. I'm not giving you chapter and verse here because too much information can be overwhelming while you're deciding if this is the business for you. The operations manual that you get access to with my oven goes into a lot more detail but for now the following should give you an excellent overview of what you need to be thinking about.

1 It's all about the dough

You want to get into this game to make money. To do that, you'll need to be smart with your dough. Get this wrong and you'll be kissing goodbye to your profit!

Frozen or Fresh?

For me, this is a "no brainer". I only use frozen dough balls that I buy in. Why? Making your own dough is time consuming, requires expensive equipment and the end result tastes no better than pizza made with thawed dough.

A little story ... 90% of people who come and talk to me about buying an oven are 100% convinced that one of their mission statements is that they will make their own dough. They think that pre-bought dough-balls are inferior to home made dough. However, after tasting one of my pizzas they all admit that the dough far exceeded their expectations and that they could see the huge benefits of buying in good quality, pre-made, consistent, frozen dough balls. For many buying a Bushman Wood-fired Oven is as much about lifestyle and choice as it is about the money. When you start a business, worrying about the dough should be at the bottom of your list of priorities. Getting more gigs and spending more time with your loved ones should be at the top of the list.

Storing your dough balls

You'll know when you've got your dough ball management right, because at the end of a trading day, you'll be left with a maximum of 10 balls that are worth about a couple of pounds in total.

With dough balls it's a case of use 'em or lose 'em. Once a dough ball has thawed, the yeast will activate and it will start to rise. If they're not used, they blend together into one big lump, which makes portion control a nightmare and they'll need knocking back to get the air out, otherwise the dough roller will shred them.

So it's really important to keep your dough balls in a refrigerator or cool box at 1–3°C and no higher, and to take 10 or so out about 20 minutes before you need them.

Any leftover dough balls could be baked as bread rolls or pitta breads that you can then freeze or a nice "end of day" touch is to make up pizzas with left over ingredients. You can box these and give them as presents to security staff or other event workers who might appreciate some free food joy in their lives. It's better than throwing it all away and it makes you friends! If however you have held them below 4°C in a cooler box you can then just carry them over to the next day or the next gig.

There's a real art to dough ball management and it's one of the areas I go into in great detail in my operations manual.

2 It's all about the oven

I love my oven! Use yours wisely, follow my instructions and you'll create great pizzas. Unfortunately, I can only guarantee results with Bushman Ovens. Others' ovens are insulated differently and the fire won't necessarily produce the same heat each time. My ovens get hot in about 45 minutes and are ready to go in under an hour. They retain heat for up to eighteen hours and are very easy to balance. Lightweight ovens on the other hand claim to come to temperature in about five to ten minutes. But beware, if they come to temperature so quickly then you will also find that they yo yo up and down in temperature and it will be difficult to hold a constant temperature which means it will be really difficult and require a huge amount of skill to cook consistent products. So here's how you would light your fire and make great pizza the Bushman way!

- Light your fire in the middle of the oven at least 20 minutes (and preferably 40 minutes) before you cook

- Push the fire to the back of the oven and sweep the oven floor before you start to cook and use a blow pipe to remove excess ash

I like to get my oven running for 45 minutes before I move the oven back into the fire basket. This ensures that I have enough heat stored in the base and the oven won't go cold. This does leave the floor really hot at this stage, so I then run it for another 20 minutes so that it can balance out. This will give you a lovely oven that will easily allow you to cook at least 50 pizzas per hour continuously. Using a medium sized oven – 85 cm internal diameter – I have personally cooked 300 pizzas in 4hrs 30 mins with a two man team and had no problems at all.

How do I know when to push the fire back? "If the dome is white, you are all right." Only push the fire back when you see the dome (inside top of the oven) go white. A white dome means a good temperature.

"If you can't see what you're cooking, you need more flame." It's easy to forget to add wood, but you can't make pizza with a cold oven. If you can't see what you're cooking, it means there's no flame in the dome. If there's no flame, you're either going to burn your pizza bottoms or have uncooked toppings. You have to get the balance right.

How to balance your oven temperature

The balance is between the temperature of the oven floor and the air inside the oven. Well-balanced ovens mean evenly cooked pizzas. You can balance the oven at any temperature; the thicker your base, the more topping you'll add and the lower the oven temperatures will need to be to cook evenly.

I run the oven floor temperature of 350 to 380°C and an air temp of between 450 and 500°C. This gives me an evenly cooked 10" thin crust pizza in about 45-90 seconds depending on the amount of topping I add.

3 It's all about the wood

I've had plenty of calls over the years from customers complaining about their ovens smoking out their whole pitch. Each call results in a long conversation.

We always end up establishing that the problem relates to the type of wood being used.

In 2009 I put my ovens through extensive testing to get the smoke exemption certification that allows them to be used anywhere in Great Britain. Finally, in April 2011, I got DEFRA approval; there's no way I would have got this exemption certificate if the ovens had smoked! I am the first UK manufacturer whose ovens were DEFRA approved which means complete peace of mind should the inspectors come knocking.

As with so many aspects of this business, there are golden rules

- Your wood's moisture content must be lower than 20%. The lower it is, the better. We run our ovens on air-dried wood with a moisture content of 15%. Check this with a damp meter.

- Keep your wood size small: 1 inch x 2 inch x 10 inch or 25mm x 50mm x 250mm. If you buy in logs with a big diameter, then be sure to split them before drying as while they may read 1% on the outside they could well be far in excess of this inside and will need further drying out.

If you are struggling with getting good dry wood then consider using   O Sole Mio from Nottingham Eco Fuels. It's a compressed beech sawdust wood with a guaranteed moisture content of 8%. It comes pre packed in easy to stack and store 18kg boxes and burns easily with a huge amount of heat. They may seem expensive but when you take into account storage and splitting costs they are more affordable than you think and with guaranteed results. There are other compressed hardwood manufacturers but the source and quality of wood is dubious. I am sure this will improve and I am testing new product all the time but my benchmark is still the O Sole Mio product which I find the best.

You can use a small amount of soft wood to get the oven fire going. But it's useless for running your oven at cooking temperature because it spits and sputters ash everywhere and can smoke like crazy when the resin burns. Avoid birch unless you can remove the bark, because it's ultra-high in tar, which smokes like mad and tastes really bad. And you will often see soot hanging like ribbons off the roof when you do use it.

How much wood do you need?

You need 10kg of wood to get one of our medium sized (85cm internal diameter) ovens hot and 3.5kg per hour to maintain oven temperature. You'll need about 1.5kg of kindling. A standard council recycling bin holds about 25kg of wood; two of them would easily cover a day's trading.

How to light the fire

Follow these steps to avoid smoke problems:

- Ensure that the kindling (very thin wood that you use to start the fire) is the driest possible

- Stack the kindling Jenga style 4 layers high and as wide as possible across the middle of the oven (about 1.2kg of kindling wood)

- Use an alcohol based lighter block or fire gel. Don't use cheap fire lighting blocks or paraffin, because they smoke big time

- Never squirt fire lighting fluid into the oven; it's explosive!!

- After about 4 minutes you'll have a roaring fire

- Add a few tinder dry hard wood fingers 25mm thick/wide

- Keep feeding in the wood fingers 2 or 3 at a time (1.5kg over a 10 minute period) to maintain a roaring, flaming fire

- Once your hot ember base has developed, start adding larger tinder dry logs. If there's no smoke you can add more logs together

- The maximum weight of wood you can burn at one time is 5kg, so don't overdo it, or you'll get… you guessed it… loads of smoke!

- After 15 minutes your oven should be burning smokeless.

Be diligent when getting your fire going. Use the right wood. Tend to your fire. Also keep in mind that if you put too much wood on the fire it will also create loads of smoke. Think of smoke as unburnt fuel, which means money going up the chimney. Remember; flames are our friends. If there are no flames, then there may well be smoke.

4 It's all about the ingredients

This is an area where you can get things wrong by going cheap and producing rubbish pizzas or going too expensive and trashing your profit. Every pizza maker has their own favourite staple ingredients and recipes. These are a few of mine:

Basic ingredients

- Frozen dough balls
- Tomato base. Thick, tasty, smooth. You need no more than 40g/2oz per pizza
- Cheese, real cheese, not the plastic stuff. I use an 80/20 blend
- Pepperoni, 8 – 10 pieces (40g) per pizza
- Ham, 40g per pizza
- Pineapple, 40g per pizza
- Brie. A standard wedge will cover 4 or 5 pizzas (1 – 3 slices each)
- Garlic butter
- Caramelised onion.

As crazy as it may seem the majority of pizzas sold in the UK are Margheritas and Pepperoni. You could just do these two and have a successful business but you'd get bored very quickly.

Food Preparation

Good organisation will save you a lot of time and money. Pre-chop your ingredients (super thin – 1mm) and store them in containers in your cooler box. Remember, only high-risk foods need to be cooled. Fresh, uncut vegetables don't need to be refrigerated.

Keep track of what you use. One of the biggest mistakes in starting out is over-estimating how much you need. Keep a note of what you sell; this will help you manage your topping ingredients. But remember that different venues will probably lead to different levels of ingredient usage.

5 Keep you pizzas super thin and crispy

Everybody has their own way of making a pizza. I make them super thin, crispy and full of flavour. Some people go for thicker bases, but these take longer to cook – we're back to transaction times and profits! A lovely, thin base is harder to handle before cooking than a thicker one, so I'm going to let you into my secrets of how to make the perfect pizza.

How to make a pizza

1. Roll the dough by hand/rolling pin or best and fastest, a dough roller

2. Spin it to dry the surface

3. Drop it on to a sparsely pre-floured bat (the wooden flat board with the handle)

4. Apply the tomato base from the centre outwards, leaving a good 10–20mm crust edge all the way round

5. Arrange the toppings so that it's easy to cut the pizza into four pieces, each with equal amounts of topping. Keep away from the crust edge

6. Add cheese, again leaving the crust edge clear

7. Lightly flour the peel (the metal "spade" for putting pizzas in the oven)

8. Slide the pizza from the bat on to the peel

9. If the pizza sticks to the bat and won't slide on to the peel, don't put it in the oven

10. Slide the pizza into the oven and cook!

MAKING THE MONEY

Finding places to trade

There are so many events, festivals and other gatherings going on that it shouldn't be too hard to find some near you. Try the following sources to get started:

- NCASS website – type it in to Google and it will come up

- The Showman's Show Directory – Google will direct you

- Google "festivals and events in (your county/city)"

- Your local council's website – events section

If you're planning to trade on a street pitch, you need to contact your local council and discuss it with them. This can take time, so there is no point in ringing them on Monday if you want to pitch on Friday!

Private/corporate events are also great gigs to get. You can use your street pitch or event pitch to market yourself for birthdays, after wedding parties etc.

Making sure you make money at organized events

I've been trading at events for more than a decade. In that time I've learnt a few home truths.

- Event organisers want to make as much money as they can

- They want to spend as little as possible

- Their "expected visitor numbers" can be way higher than the actual footfall

- They sometimes over promise on the level of advertising they're doing to promote the event

That might all sound quite grim, but if you play your cards right, you'll make the correct choices about the events you go for (and make some money). Paying £10 to be at a small, local function that guarantees 300 people and 3 food outlets is a good move. In my opinion it is far better than paying £800 to be at a new, free festival that expects 5000 a day; bad weather will drastically reduce the actual numbers at an event like this. And you could be left with rotting stock and an empty till.

Rather than paying a fixed fee, look for events that work on commission and take a percentage of your turnover. If an event charges a fixed fee, don't be afraid of explaining that commission could well work better for them if they get a good turnout; you sell more, so they get paid more. If they decline, you might be better off not doing the event.

Remember if the deal sounds too good to be true, it probably is!

Always work out the number of pizzas you'll need to make in order to break even. If a festival is charging you £2,000 for 2 days plus 20% of your gross takings, you need to know that you can make enough pizzas to make money. If you can't, don't be afraid to walk away.

Be proactive

Most of the time when doing a function you will be allocated a pitch.

Of course if you have done the gig before you will know where the best pitch is but if it's your first time you are going to learn the hard way. And that can be expensive.

So you need to be sure that you are proactive. By that I mean if you are not doing any sales, then move!

Of course if you are working on a commission basis then it's in the organiser's best interest that you do move.

You may find that at some all day and night gigs during the day you need to be in one place and at night you need to be in another. So don't be shy, you are not there to look pretty you are there to make money!

If it turns out to be a good gig you will know for next year where you need to be and make sure you get that pitch.

Making sure you make money at private events

My favourite booking is a private party. I get a guaranteed fee for a set number of pizzas. If I stay late or cook more, I charge a pre-agreed amount. Easy. Certain. Profitable! But there's a knack to getting your pricing right for your function. You'll need to consider mileage, late-hours payment, number of people, pizzas offered and expenses. And don't forget you may need to provide tables and chairs as well. For some operators this is a tidy and lucrative add on although I personally don't offer this.

To get a closer look at how I make money catering for private events, sign up for my free, detailed 11-page report "A Day in the Life of a Wedding Catererer" at

www.bushmanwoodfiredovens.co.uk/dayinthelife.

Event types and how to adjust your menu to suit them

1 High volume functions

When you're busy, under pressure and have a lot of hungry people to feed, a small menu is a beautiful and profitable thing.

At a music festival, for example, people want great food fast; keep them waiting too long and you'll lose them.

I often have just two options at a big event; a Margherita and a pepperoni. Nothing else.

I promise you, if you have a long queue of people waiting it's best to reduce your offering to your most profitable and most desired pizzas.

Remember that 80% of your profit will come from 20% of your products – so if you are flat out there's not much point in serving the 80% of product that only give you 20% of profit.

2 Medium volume functions

You will still have quite a few people looking for great food, but you can afford to stretch to four options, as long as you always have a Margherita in there. You and your customers will have a little more time, so more choice is ok!

3 Private parties

If you are catering for large numbers (200+) then either reduce down the menu to two choices or create a buffet. I have now served 600 people over the course of a lunch / afternoon, buffet style. It's hard work as you are making pizza as fast as you can. But it's great fun and because it's a buffet you cut each pizza into six slices. So if your oven capacity is 50 pizza per hour, then after 2 hours everyone has had something to eat – happy days!

For small and cozy parties (60-100 people) allow more choice when it comes to the menu – I just love these types of event. They're very lucrative and rewarding.

Why?

- They pay irrespective of the weather

- You get your fee up front

- You can build in an overtime or "over numbers" payment to cover yourself for a later finish or guests who want more, more, more

- You can be creative and add some theatre and flair to your pizzas!

- You can push your brand by doing brilliant food while being fun and funky (if you're good, people will remember you)

4 Children's functions

Kids are strange creatures; they tend to like Margherita or Pepperoni...and nothing much else! So think carefully about keeping it really simple.

5 Themed parties and "going posh"

Your wonderful oven is more than just a pizza oven. You can cook anything in it, such as suckling pig, scallops, lamb, naan bread/chapati. So, expand your horizons! Why not consider

- Greek nights (moussaka, kofta, lamb pittas, kleftico)

- Indian nights (naan, chapati, roti, tandoori lamb/chicken/beef)

- Moroccan nights (tagine, skewers)

- Fish nights (delicacies of the sea)

- Veggie nights (stuffed peppers, tomatoes, mushrooms & halloumi cheese)

If you've got a discerning clientele, you might want to up-spec your menu to "go posh". Here's a menu I've used (and charged very good money for):

Starter
Sealed scallops in their shells
Main
Rare roast beef in a pitta wrap with Mediterranean vegetables
done in balsamic vinegar, or coleslaw with a
horseradish and sweet pepper sauce
Dessert
Tarte Tatin with apple, apricot or peach & slow baked
apple crumble with a fresh custard

If this sort of menu whets your appetite, you should consider booking on a course at Manna from Devon's wood-fired oven cookery course. David and Holly Jones will really look after you and will give you the skills and confidence to get so much more out of your oven. Visit www.mannafromdevon.com for more information and consider picking up a copy of David and Holly's book on Cooking with Wood-fired Ovens. For other sample recipes visit the Bushman Wood-fired Ovens website.

6 Making money at local markets

Taking a pitch at a local market can be a nice little earner but it will never make you rich. I use these events as more of a marketing opportunity, so that prospective private bookings, weddings and corporates can come and see the trailer and oven in action.

Since most markets get under way quite early (and you have to be there from the start), it's a good idea to have two price boards ready, because the mornings may be slower for you.

You can offer two different menus too - breakfast type foods in the morning and then pizzas at lunch time/afternoon.

In the morning try offering croissants, muffins, teacakes and pain au chocolate up until about 11.30. You can also do breakfast baps - bacon and sausages cook fantastic in the wood-fired oven. A bacon bap served with relish is a great way to go, and also works well at weddings for the 2am breakfast session, you can literally serve 50 baps in no time at all.

From 11:30am onwards pull the breakfast boards in and go for broke with your pizzas. You should be busy from midday to 2.30pm, earning some good money. As with very large events and functions, it's best to keep your pizza menu simple for these kind of pitches as you need to turn things around quickly.

7 Festivals

If you're not afraid of some hard graft, then festivals might be for you. I've done 1,200 pizzas in 3 days from a medium size oven with three people working flat out between 11am and 7pm, very tiring, but good earnings.

If the festival goes on into the evening, you get two hits at the customers, who are around for lunch and dinner.

Event set up and take down

There's a lot to think about when you are starting out and you will want to make your life as simple and routine as possible. It's a really good idea to document your set up and close down procedures for a typical event. Don't forget to include food preparation, setting up the trailer or vehicle, and delegating clear responsibilities for each staff member.

THE SHACK REVOLUTION

FESTIVALS

bushman wood fired ovens

MARKETING YOUR BUSINESS

So you have your oven, you have your unit and you've worked out your concept. Now you need to let everyone know about your business!

But be aware, you can waste a lot of money marketing your pizza business badly.

This is what I've learned about affordable, effective marketing:

Work out your brand

A brand is more than a look. It's who you are, how you operate, what your values are. It can reference your concept (sourdough pizza), your mission (healthy fast food) or your customers (day trippers). It's the principles you run your business by and the way you want your business to look.

Create a look and use it on everything

It's worth developing a "look" for your business.

Particular fonts, colours and a good logo will go a long way towards giving you a professional identity.

You don't necessarily have to hire a graphic designer or a big design agency to do this, I know people who have got friends and family to come up with ideas that have been really great.

If you don't have the creative bug, find a small, hungry branding company that wants to do a good job for a fair price. They are out there. There are also some good online design "agencies" e.g. fiverr.com.

Make sure your logo is on everything; banners, flyers, menus, business stationery, even your trailer/van if you have the budget (and I suggest that you make provision).

Pizza boxes, plates and napkins can all proudly carry your logo too.

Have a website

People like to go online and have a look at you, so you should at least have a "shop window" of a site that gives contact details, where you trade regularly and what your ethos is. Get some good photos up as well! But make sure that any website developer you use, uses the WordPress platform. It will save you much trouble and stress later down the line. Also make sure you own the copyright to the website and not the web designer. This will give you the freedom to use whoever you wish in the future to make alterations and it can be done quite cheaply whereas if you use their own platform it will lead to nightmares down the line. It's also critical to make sure any website you build or get built works *beautifully* on mobiles and tablets – at the time of writing over 65% of Google searches are now made on mobile devices. and this is only going to increase.

Facebook

Social media is also a great way to create a buzz for your business. Make sure your pizza business has an online presence like a blog, Facebook page or Twitter account. Facebook is becoming more and more important for any mobile caterer as it gives the customer an easy quick reference to find out what you are offering. Facebook I would say is becoming more important than owning a website. It's also a lot easier to set up and manage. As you grow your business, Facebook marketing will prove more and more important both in driving new traffic and creating credibility. Be sure to get some glowing testimonials from your happy customers.

Have handouts on your unit

I personally favour postcards. They need to carry your logo, your contact details and your website. If your customers have enjoyed your pizza, they might just take a handful and give them to their friends or book you for themselves for a private party or special. Business cards are useful too and can work in the same way as postcards and flyers.

Loyalty cards

If you're going to trade in one place regularly (say, a market on a Saturday), then hand out loyalty cards. You could stamp cards for people every time they buy a pizza, then once they've collected enough stamps give them a discount, a free side/drink or even a free pizza if you're feeling really generous.

All they have to do is give you their email address and mobile number. You promise never to pass these on and only to use them to let your customers know when you're in town and what your specials are.

You could also offer loyalty cardholders a discounted price if they book you for an event.

Google Adwords

To generate business from an online presence, you need to be a top hit in the Google search results for wood-fired pizza in your local area.

Our wood-fired pizza oven has arrived! - The Shack Revolution
www.theshackrevolution.co.uk/blog/our_wood-fired_pizza_oven_has_arrived/ ▾
BOOK A TABLE Hereford: 01432 509464. Menu, About, Meet ... Jay from Bushman Wood Fired Ovens dropped off our sexy new pizza oven this morning, hurrah!

It works and it's not hard. Get on to Google and research this (or sign up for my subscription newsletter for the latest pizza-business specific marketing advice). If you go down the ad route you can target your market very accurately and give your business a big lift. This technique may sound expensive but in most cases it is cheaper than advertising in the local media.

Get networking

Visit your local town or shopping centre, park your van and give out your postcards or flyers. Chat to people. Offer to provide food at charity events (where you can give out promotional material).

Tell all your friends on Facebook. Set up a "Pizza" page and get them all to Like it.

Post information online (via Facebook, twitter or a blog) about up-coming events, plus photos from past events you've done.

If there are any food festivals in your area make sure you attend - let people in your local area know you are available to cater for parties, festivals and other events.

Do whatever you need to do to ensure people know who you are, what you do and where they can find you!

Marketing videos

We are currently running a trial of a video media presentation on our trailer. In this video we talk about how the honesty box ordering system works, but after that there is a video compilation of the different types of functions that we do and we invite people to take a card and get back to us if they would like to book us for an event.

SUCCESS STORIES: CONVERTED VEHICLES

Sole Luna Wood Fired Pizza

My experience with Jay and Bushman Wood-Fired Ovens was really amazing. From my first meeting with him I realised that I have next to me, not a salesman who wants to sell his product, but a person who gave me all the information and advice to run a business and the steps to grow and to get where I wanted to be, always with the smile on his face and the same great attitude.

Without his help and advice my business wouldn't exist. I would highly recommend him and his great products.

Daniel Popa, Sole Luna Wood Fired Pizza

Well Kneaded Food

Jay Emery puts 150% minimum into everything he does – from oven design to customer service. From the moment you arrive at his outback bush recreation in Kidderminster, to launch, through to product development you are in great hands. Ovens last for ages. We're 5 years in and it's still burning bright. We couldn't have launched without him.

We recommend him everywhere we go!

Brigit Callaghan, Well Kneaded Food

The Pizza Oven

In 2012 my friend Helen and I decided to embark into the world of Street Food. Wood fired pizza was a passion that was shared by Jay Emery at Bushman Wood-Fired Ovens. Thanks to the knowledge and advice (initially shared in the yurt at Bushman HQ) and fantastic hand-made ovens, The Pizza Oven was born and has grown to be a fun and successful street food business with 3 vans visiting 12 regular pitches a week in Sussex and a diary full of festivals, weddings and events at weekends.

Jay's advice has been invaluable in giving us the head start and advice along the way. He is passionate and knowledgeable about wood fired cooking and has always been willing to give help and advice.

Thank you, Jay.

Helen and Emma, The Pizza Oven

The Travelling Pizzeria

The Travelling Pizzeria is a stylish, quirky and professional Devon-based mobile catering business that specialises in wood fired, artisan pizza.

We've just received a Taste of the West Gold Award. We like buying local produce and coming up with innovative pizzas but recognize that a key part of creating a perfect pizza is the oven.

Our Bushman Wood Fired Oven is side-mounted into a beautiful Citroen H Van, so customers see the wood fire as their pizzas are cooked. In all weather conditions and circumstances the oven keeps its temperature brilliantly.

As well as creating a great oven for us, when we first visited Jay he was generous with his time and gave us some invaluable advice. Without his initial help and input we believe that our business would not have developed so rapidly or successfully.

Jonathan & Julie Dandy, The Travelling Pizzeria

Bare Bones Pizza

Finding out about Jay and Bushman Wood-Fired Ovens was pretty essential for us starting up Bare Bones Pizza in 2014. During our research phase, we saw a lot of businesses we liked using Bushman Ovens, so knew that we had to have the same to achieve the high quality we were after. After meeting Jay, you quickly find out that he isn't someone who just builds fantastic ovens, he is extremely passionate about the mobile pizza business that his ovens can provide the basis for a successful business for all his customers. We had a lot of meetings with Jay, as well as contacting him regularly for advice. These were invaluable when setting up our business; from finding suppliers, to a list of contacts, to helping us find some of our first gigs. Almost two years down the line and we are still in touch with Jay, with him coming to see how we are getting on at some of our events. We owe Jay a big thank you.

Mike Evans, Bare Bones Pizza

Pizzazz

I first met Jay on a cold and wet March day. In two hours my plan for a garden pizza oven had changed into something much bigger – running a mobile pizzeria. Although I didn't dive right in there and then, all of the advice that I got from Jay on how to setup a small business proved itself over time to be straightforward, practical and from a real life perspective. I don't think there was any part of Jay's original 'blueprint' that didn't add value or relevance to the way in which our business is operating today. So all credit to Mr Emery for sharing his insights with all his clients in such an open and honest fashion. Thank you Jay!

Alex Jaggers, Pizzazz, London

Bordoli's Wood Fired Kitchen

The most important decision that myself and my wife Cheryl made when deciding to start a pizza business was in choosing to buy our oven from Jay Emery. Having Jay's help and advice through the whole process was invaluable. Right from designing the layout of the van, training day, making pizzas, serving customers, dealing with all the red tape involved with food industry, he just made everything effortless. I don't think there is an

aspect of this business he cannot help you with. After sales service is second to none, even 2 years down the line he has helped me get out of trouble. In my opinion if you are serious about getting into this business you'll not go wrong getting this man on your side.

Dominic and Cheryl Owen, Bordoli's Wood Fired Kitchen

Flaming Indulgence

I had a dream and have passion but what I did not have was the knowledge or expertise to implement my dream. Until I met Jay whose vast experience and incredible insight into the wood-fired pizza world allowed me to create my new business venture. Without his business guide it simply would not have happened. The oven is my pride and joy and as Flaming Indulgence grows I have been given the opportunity to not only have successful business, but a better quality of life. Thanks Jay!

Rhona Quarm, Flaming Indulgence Wood Fired Pizza

The Big Blu

I bought a wood fired oven from Jay 4 years ago and I have to say that it is not only a beautiful and elegant design but without doubt a brilliant oven, form and function combined. If I had to recommend one investment in a start up pizza business it would be a Bushman Oven.

Chris Percy-Davis, The Big Blu

Janet's Wood Fired Pizza

Thank you you very much for helping me set up a wood fired catering business. From when I first saw you and your oven at the seminar in Wellingborough I was inspired to start my own business. When I first left school in 1987, I trained as a chef but gave it up after three years because of low wages and long hours. Having my own wood-fired catering business still means long hours but the money is soooo much better!

Dave and Janet Franklin, Janet's Wood Fired Pizza

SUCCESS STORIES: HORSE BOXES

Wild Bake

Back in 2013 I realised there was a need for some good quality wood-fired pizza down in Cornwall. I did some research into clay ovens. Jay at Bushman Wood-Fired Ovens was the first person I contacted, after a very exciting chat I tore up the list of other oven suppliers.....I knew this was the company that would help me move my business forward. I'm now nearly four years in and haven't ever looked back! Without Jay's enthusiasm and knowledge I don't think Wild Bake would be where it is today.

If you are thinking of getting into the wood fired pizza industry, I would highly recommend The Bushman Oven Company.

Lewis Cole, Wild Bake

Wild Fire Pizza

Once I had chosen Jay's oven to buy I was amazed by the amount of after sales service he was prepared to put in. During the build of my business I encountered many problems which I had to turn to Jay's wealth of experience to help me solve. He was always available and willing to help. It would have been a much harder job if I didn't have his help along the way.

John King, Wild Fire Pizza

SUCCESS STORIES: NO-FRILLS TRAILERS
Doughkitchen

Doughkitchen spent a great deal of time searching the Republic of Ireland, UK and France to find an oven that met our specific mobile catering requirements. In the end there was only one oven that stood out above all the rest. The Bushman Wood-Fired Oven of course! Craftsmanship, durability and the customer service are all aspects of both the purchase and continued service that exceeded our expectations.

The startup guide on how to run a mobile wood-fired oven successfully is worth its weight in gold and we often refer back to it (or the bible as we call it!). As an end to end service, we would happily recommend Bushman Wood-Fired Ovens (in particular their founder Jay Emery).

Doughkitchen went for a bespoke oven and one that could rotate 360 degrees, so as to suit any function/event we attended.

Looking forward to doing business again with Bushman Wood-Fired Ovens in the future.

David McFadden, Doughkitchen

Maxine's Mobile Pizza

I bought my oven from Jay in August 2011 and my business has grown rapidly, starting as a weekend hobby to what it is now – a full time business employing staff, enabling me to give up the day job 18 months after I first 'hit the street'.

Jay's support throughout the past five years and especially at the beginning, has been invaluable. At the start of my venture Jay provided everything from ideas (a wonderful mind map!) to where to buy the best equipment and which trade body to join. And Jay's on-going support has been wonderful. Just knowing Jay is there to run ideas past, chat over any issues and that he is always happy to talk gives great piece of mind.

Two key areas Jay would often talk about is 'always think of ways to improve service and expand the business' and I have done just that, taking my business from what was once a street food vendor to full catering services for weddings and private hires. I have travelled all over the UK, from the west coast of Wales, the islands and Highlands of Scotland and regularly visit London. I have also made sure I can cater for all requirements from vegetarians, vegans, Halal meats, gluten free…

It's hard work, let's not ignore that! But the one thing I can always rely on has been my oven, always providing wonderful pizzas in all weathers! Five years down the line it still looks great, and I wouldn't change it for anything!

I would highly recommend Jay's ovens to anyone thinking of starting a business in pizza street food.

Maxine Pearson, Maxine's Mobile Pizza

Pizza Monkey

From first meeting Jay, his enthusiasm, work ethic and passion for what he does was infectious. What was even more striking was his desire to pass on best practice and lessons learnt over the years to ensure my new business got off to the best start possible. Jay went out of his way to ensure that me as his customer was fully versed on how to run a pizza business effectively and efficiently and didn't fall short on the common mistakes new starts often make. Jay gave invaluable tips, tricks and industry knowledge in order to create the successful pizza business I operate today.

Nick Higgs, Pizza Monkey

Cibo Fresco

The service we received from Bushman Wood-Fired Ovens was exceptional! We could not have asked for a better team to guide us through the buying and installation process. Jay's experience and patience served us well. His local market knowledge is invaluable, his guidance and resources were key to setting up our business. Jay is a true professional and the oven in a class by itself.

Polly Wilson, Cibo Fresco

Hadrian's Pizza

Like many people my wife and I first had the idea of making wood fired pizza while on holiday in Italy, we had been to festivals in the UK and seen mobile pizza ovens and having tasted the real deal we knew that recreating this experience in the UK was what we wanted to do.

But with no previous experience in catering let alone pizza making, how could we do it?

We researched the options and spoke to several oven manufacturers, then we spoke to Jay. The first thing which made us think we had found our man was Jay's enthusiasm and knowledge of the industry we wanted to be part of. The fact that Jay was willing to share his hard won knowledge meant that in the space of a few minutes our dream suddenly became a reality.

We left our seminar in March 2012 grinning and full of ideas. As we're living overseas we didn't collect our oven until November 2014, in the meantime we had read Jay's manual from cover to cover many times and had soaked up the information.

Now with our medium oven and no frills trailer we were ready to make pizza! Using Jay's blueprint we had a fantastic first year, we were turning up at events, selling pizzas and making money. Naturally we made some mistakes which we quickly learnt from and we knew Jay was never far away if we needed some advice.

Fast forward to summer 2016 and we have a wall planner packed with events and a dozen weddings already booked in for 2017, one of our biggest problems now is what to do when we we have several enquiries for the same weekend. It's great to catch up with Jay as we did a few weeks ago when he made a running repair to our trailer and as always he was thinking of the next development in wood fired pizza catering. Maybe one day we will need a second oven, if we do there's only one place we will go!

Dan Stephenson, Hadrian's Pizza

SUCCESS STORIES: COMPACT KITCHENS
Nonnina's Wood Fired Pizzas

I personally spent 6 months researching and looking for the best quality pizza ovens before investing any money into our new business venture and one name kept on shouting back at me "Bushman". We booked a seminar with Jay and after an informal chat, a demonstration on how the ovens work and tasting the pizzas, we knew at that point we were with the right guy with the right product. I asked Jay if I could buy one of his compact kitchens ASAP. Two months later we are now trading and our business is turning over an increasing profit every week. Not only do you get the best quality pizza oven you can buy, you also have Jay assisting you if required. This guy not only manufactures his own ovens he also offers you his wealth of knowledge within the catering sector. We are doing so well in our early days of trading because we have been guided by Jay. He is successful so we've decided to be a carbon copy of him. Use his business model and use a Bushman oven. Not once have we had any doubts about our investment. Thank you Jay for your help, support and advice. Much appreciated.

Neil Baddeley
Nonnina's Wood Fired Pizzas

Pizza-Ria

We went to see Jay at one of his free seminar sessions. Jay was clearly extremely knowledgeable, both making and using his brilliant oven and was more than happy to pass on his wealth of experience. Jay's enthusiasm was limitless and he was obviously passionate about his product and that anyone who bought into his brand would go on and be successful.

The after sales service was second to none, Jay's wisdom, in his book is priceless, paving the way for the novice into the pizza catering industry to avoid the many pitfalls.

Pizza-Ria is going from strength to strength confident in the knowledge that their oven set up is the best money can buy and that there is an endless pool of knowledge at the end of the phone. Jay is an inspiration and has been a pleasure to meet and do business with.

Rob and Maria Marshall, Pizza-Ria

SUCCESS STORIES: COOKERY SCHOOLS

Manna from Devon

Here at Manna from Devon Cooking School we've been working with Jay Emery & Bushman Wood-Fired Ovens since 2009. What can we say? We love Jay and his passion for what he does & we love our ovens as do our students when they taste the incredible food that comes out of them.

David and Holly Jones
Manna From Devon Cooking School

SUCCESS STORIES: STREET FOOD EVENTS
Digbeth Dining Club

Back in August 2012, we started Digbeth Dining Club, Birmingham's first weekly street food event.

Unlike today, the popularity of street food had not even registered in the Midlands and Jay with the Bushman's Pizza brand was one of our first traders and with a successful first event the future looked rosy. It wasn't. In our first year, it was hard going with traders at best doing no more than 40-50 covers. Without the support of the likes of Jay to turn up and believe in the event in that first year, despite the financial drawbacks for traders, lack of customers and what seemed like a year of cold weather we seemed to have, DDC would not be where it is today.

In September 2013, we won Best Event at the British Street Food Awards and since then have won multiple awards. DDC is recognised as one of the reasons for Birmingham being recognised as a food destination with a huge turnout each week and traders all now selling covers in the hundreds. We also now have similar events running across the Midlands with over 50 DDC traders on our books. Without the work of founding members like Jay though, none of this would have been possible.

Jack Brabant, Digbeth Dining Club

SUCCESS STORIES: RESTAURANTS & TAKE-AWAYS

La Favorita Delivered

Meeting Jay was a huge turning point – our conversations ultimately inspired my 'aha moment' and with his help we have transformed our business. We worked with Jay to design and build our own oven and this one-of-a-kind oven was built, amazingly, in 12 weeks and it immediately made La Favorita Delivered both scalable and profitable. His 'failure is not an option' approach matches our drive and determination and that is why he continues to play an integral part in our brand's success. We consider Jay and his team an extension of ours and as such we know we are extremely fortunate to have his steadfast support as we work hard to realise our vision.

Kenny Scott, Owner/CEO La Favorita Delivered

The Shack Revolution

Using Jay's ovens has really made the initial step of setting up our first restaurant that little bit easier. All the support and help he has given us has meant we have been able to focus on all the other aspects of the restaurant. The oven itself is a testament to the team's hard work and passion.

Rich Manning, The Shack Revolution

Stable Hearth Wood-Fired Foods and Artisan Pizzeria

I I first met Jay of Bushman Wood-Fired Ovens in April 2013 after initially speaking to him on the phone (for some time, may I add!) with the view to opening a wood fired food business. Since our first conversation in March 2013 I can honestly say that I have never once questioned my decision in purchasing one of Jay's wood fired ovens (it is now August 2016).

When you purchase an oven off Jay, you don't just get a fantastic Bushman oven, you also get your own personal helpline from Jay himself. It's been a relief to have been able to set up my new wood fired food business Stable Hearth, and know that I can call on Jay's expertise to answer any questions I have, or to solve any operational problems or queries that I may have!

That's the good thing about dealing with Bushman Wood-Fired Ovens; Jay is not just an oven maker, he is also an owner/operator of a wood fired pizza operation and he doesn't just cut you off once he has sold you an oven. He's prepared to supply you with an oven that meets your requirements and business needs. He knows the pitfalls and positives of running a business that is centred around supplying a product from a wood fired oven and you can call upon him at any time afterwards for his expertise in this matter. For anyone looking to purchase a wood fired oven I would definitely advise them to speak to Jay as he could stop you making and regretting a bad decision... If you go to one of his seminars then prepare for it by taking the time to write down all your queries and questions that you may have on running a business and oven in this specialised food service sector of the hospitality industry.

As for his oven, I am currently running a medium sized oven in my business. The quality of the oven matches and compliments the quality of the food that Stable Hearth is providing our customers. The oven is a focal point that our customers see when they walk in, and it's been a rewarding experience to be able to cook on it.

Nicholas Thexton, Stable Hearth Wood-Fired Foods and Artisan Pizzeria

Site Pizzeria

We first met Jay after stumbling across his business whilst scouring the net looking for someone who could make a pizza oven to meet the requirements of our restaurant 'Site' being in a conservation area.

During our first meeting it was blatantly evident that we'd struck lucky! Jay's passion and knowledge of all things pizza along with his willingness to share all his experience and expertise is quite overwhelming.

We had naively thought we'd buy the oven from him, start making and selling pizzas and that'd be that. Easy!

Even now, two years on we sincerely believe that had we not happened upon Jay without a doubt we would not have the successful business that Site is. From the layout of all the equipment, lighting the fire, which wood to use, suppliers, choosing ingredients, costing, recipes, presentation, marketing, staff training, the list is endless where Jay's knowledge and input is hugely valuable.

You don't just buy a pizza oven from Jay you buy the steps and support to really get a successful business up and running and remain consistent. I'm happy I was naive. I'd have never have done it otherwise but I know now it's not as easy as you think, really not easy at all but with Jay's oven and support, dedication and hard work it can be successful from the start! Jay is a one stop shop for anyone considering running a pizza business and I can't recommend him highly enough!

Thanks Jay!

Natalie Barrass, Site, Todmordon

Restaurant Sat Bains

The work we do at Restaurant Sat Bains with Rooms is very exacting. That includes the menus we create and produce here. The technical equipment that facilitates our dishes ranges from ultra modern cooking kit to good old fashioned preserving and fermenting in jars, but everything we do is founded on one goal – flavour.

One of my favourite flavour profiles is the smoky, charred fullness of wood smoke. From aubergines to apples to slow cooked meats, wood smoke just imparts that mellowness to certain dishes. It can't be replicated by anything else.

I've known Jay Emery, the founder of Bushman Wood Fired Ovens, since 2009. Our first joint exercise was to design and build a small wood-burning oven that would sit in our garden next to our then Development Kitchen. We used it for vegetables, fruit and meat and it taught us just how flexible wood fired cooking was for us. The next step then was to somehow incorporate a larger one in our main restaurant kitchen, which was no easy task as space was so tight.

We also needed a radical solution to the problem of the extra heat in the cooking environment. By removing an existing window and mounting the belly of the oven outside the building, we managed to minimise the residual heat inside the kitchen. Bushman also developed an ingenious method of removing all the ash and mess from the back of the oven, which helps keep our kitchen spotless and ash free. Necessity is the mother of invention, and Jay certainly delivered on both counts!

However, what our two Bushman ovens have delivered as far as our guests are concerned is just that more intense, ancient flavour to some of our menu ingredients and dishes and the feedback has been phenomenal. Bushman Wood Fired Ovens have brought an exciting new dimension to the restaurant menus.

Sat Bains, Restaurant Sat Bains

RULES AND REGULATIONS TO BE AWARE OF

This might not be as sexy as actually running or marketing your business, but it's the bit you have to get right. A good, well-planned business will be more efficient and more profitable. It's also less likely to get into trouble with the authorities, which can get expensive or end your business before it has even begun!

This list of things to consider is not meant to scare or put you off becoming a mobile caterer. A lot of what is asked for is common sense and every single requirement on this list is very achievable with the right knowledge and approach.

Public/Environmental Health & Safety – what you need to get right

There's a lot of legislation that applies to mobile caterers and street trading and it changes regularly.

My best advice is treat what follows as guidelines to consider and make sure you contact your local council to get the most up to date information, simultaneously putting you straight in their good books!

1. Registering and certification

If you sell food you need to have registered your business with the U.K. Local Authority at least 28 days before you wish to start trading. It's a really good idea to be on the front foot with your local authority. If you have a good rapport with them, they can be very helpful.

There are tips that will make life a little easier. For example, when you are being inspected, explain that all preparation is done on site in your unit. This means there's no need to have your home inspected as well.

2. Food safety management system – HACP

HACCP (Hazard Analysis Critical Control Point) is the systematic preventative approach to food safety. Basically, in order to trade legally you'll need to produce adequate documents and records that show you know how to run your food safety management system.

You'll need to cover the following HACCP areas in your Operating Manual:

- Recipes
- Your produce delivery/collection schedule
- Records of delivered product condition
- Set up/break down procedures
- Records of delivering products conditions
- Allergens listings for all pizzas
- Records of freezer and cool box temperatures
- A copy of your Risk Assessment for your unit and your operations plan
- A note of your first aid kit contents and checking schedule
- A cleaning schedule that covers daily, weekly and deep cleaning processes
- A written record of training certification

3. Food handlers' certification

It's a good idea to have Level 2 Food Hygiene certificates for all staff, but you'll only pass an event inspection if staff demonstrate they understand this issue.

Your best bet is to get yourself on your local council's Food Hygiene course. That way, you show willing and start a good relationship with the people who are going to be regulating your unit. NCASS also offer Food Hygiene courses, so you could use them as an alternative.

4. Maintaining cold temperatures

Gas or electric refrigerators are normally necessary to maintain cold temperatures in the summer. If you intend to only use insulated containers (cool boxes) they'll need to be of high insulation efficiency (as defined by British Standard). They must maintain foods below 8°C, and preferably below 5°C; but you'll need lower temperatures than that anyway for your dough. You need to check which of your ingredients need to be kept cold (e.g. salad, cooked meat) and then make sure you comply with the "below 8°C" rule.

5. Preventing contamination

There are quite a few points to consider here. Raw and cooked foods obviously need to be kept separate at all times and all staff need to wear protective clothing that they can change regularly. Long hair needs to be tied up and ideally put in a hair net or hat. You'll need to regularly wipe down your working surfaces with an anti bacterial, food safe cleaner.

6. Hand washing

The law requires washing and drying facilities for hands. Alternative hand hygiene methods won't be good enough. Food handlers must regularly wash their hands thoroughly with hot soapy water. You'll need to factor this in to your unit design (or re-design).

You need a separate basin for hand washing. You'll need controllable hot and cold water, soap, a nailbrush, a supply of paper towels and a towel bin. If you can't squeeze a hand basin in to your unit, you can usually use a clean plastic bowl, as long as you have hot and cold water.

7. Washing up

You'll need a sink big enough to wash your biggest food preparation equipment item. It'll need to be protected from the weather. You'll also need a hot and cold water supply.

If you're washing food (salad, for example) you either need a separate sink or a large, clean plastic/stainless steel bowl.

8. Floors and walls

All your flooring throughout must be level and non-slip where possible. You must keep it clean and it must be washable. Walls also need to be washable. If you're preparing food next to tent style walls, they need to be easy to clean. It's best to have a fireproof piece of stainless steel on the floor in front of the oven mouth. Sometimes you will be emptying hot coals out of the oven and they may drop. If the floor is plastic, vinyl or fiberglass it's going to burn. So stainless steel checker plate is about the best option.

9. Water supply

Plan this carefully for every event you trade at! Some places have portable water and some don't. If they don't, you'll need to bring full water containers. If they do, you'll need to know if you can connect into the supply or whether you need containers.

If you use containers, you'll need to clean them inside and out regularly.

You're not allowed to tip foul water into the drainage system. If your venue has no foul water disposal system, you'll need to have waste water containers that are clearly marked. Check you've got a method of safely tipping your waste water in to your containers. Be sure to mark the tops of the dirty water containers so that you don't mix them up with the clean water ones.

10. Waste

You need waste bins with tight fitting lids and bag liners. You need to tie your waste bags regularly and put them out of the way to reduce the number of flies. If the venue doesn't offer waste collection, you'll need to deal with your waste yourself. Think through how you're going to do that.

11. Lighting and power

You'll need enough supply and plug points for artificial lighting and your fridge (if you have one). All electrical connections and adaptations should be made by a competent electrician, in accordance with the latest edition of IEE's Wiring Regulations. You'll also need to have an electrical certificate.

12. Storage

All your foodstuffs need to be kept at least 0.5m off the ground, out of sunlight and away from damp.

Keep your storage area tidy as messiness is often picked up on during inspections.

13. Ventilation & lighting

Although not exactly a compliance issue, it's worth mentioning here. In the summer months it can get really warm in the close confines of a van or stand-in trailer so think about mounting a fan somewhere to keep you cool. Also think about putting some skylights in the roof. The ventilated ones that they have in caravans are a good idea as they can be opened and closed as needed.

We have also had cases where the Environmental Health Officer has insisted that there is a free air supply into your vehicle or stand-in trailer to ensure that there is enough airflow so that the cab does not fill up with smoke. I therefore recommend that you have a minimum 20 square-inch ventilation unit somewhere in the trailer.

If you are running gas bottles then these need to have an outside mounting or be mounted in their own flameproof, fireproof box.

14. Health and safety

The law says you must act to eliminate all workplace risks that might affect the safety of your staff and others (such as the pizza-buying public or anyone who happens to be on or around your work area).

To avoid tricky questions from health and safety inspectors, it is best to have a written Risk Assessment that covers your whole operation and your working practices. Again NCASS can help you with this. As part of your membership they will supply you with a wood-fired oven specific risk assessment but if you want to do it yourself here are the things you need to do.

There are three main things to cover off for each risk area:

- A description of each of the risks or potential risks

- A note of how you're preventing or reducing each one

- An assessment of how the risk looks before and after your reduction measures

Risk areas you might need to assess could include everything from safe construction/dismantling/moving of your unit, slip/trip hazards to young people at work and fire hazards.

You absolutely must have a CO_2 fire extinguisher and a fire blanket (this is a minimum — ask your local fire prevention officer for advice that's right for your unit) and a fully stocked and up-to-date first aid kit with hygiene approved, bright coloured plasters.

15. Stay safe on the road

By the time you've packed up after an event and hit the road, you'll be shattered. Your adrenaline will keep you going for 45 minutes, but then you'll begin to feel tired. After 75 minutes, you'll be struggling to focus and you'll be a potential danger.

It's crucial that you plan your post-event rest carefully to avoid serious problems. Remember, you're towing a trailer or driving a big, heavy van and it's hard work. Better to stop and sleep than to have an accident.

And if you're really shattered it's worth checking into a service station motel or setting an alarm. Recently we were done for overstaying our welcome in a service station car park. Two and a half hours is the maximum. The fine was more than the cost of checking into the hotel.

I have turned my trailer over on the motorway late at night. Believe me when I say it's not fun! The clean up bill was no joy either.

WHAT'S NEXT?

If you've read this far and you're still excited about setting up a mobile pizza business, we'd love to help you with your next steps. Assuming that you have a minimum of £15k available to set up your business, it's time to give us a call and book a discovery seminar in our workshops/showroom. Just give us a ring on +44 1905 621636.

Now you may be thinking that this book contains everything you need to know to run a successful pizza business and there's no point coming to see us. I need to let you know that I could have made this book three or four times as long again with twice as much detail but I didn't. There's no point sharing the minutiae of frozen dough ball management or the ten critical questions to ask an event organizer before you book an event, until you're sure this is the business for you.

Running a mobile catering business can be a great way to make a living but learning the ropes by yourself takes time. You can do this the hard way and learn from your own mistakes, or you can get the shortcuts from Bushman Wood-fired Ovens and a Bushman Oven. Wouldn't it be great to get a sense check from the experts? We really believe you shouldn't have to do this alone. Come and see us in Kidderminster. If nothing else you'll get to taste the best pizza of your life.

Remember, when you buy your oven from Bushman Wood-fired Ovens you will be getting:

- The best oven in the business; reliable, efficient and easy to use

- Personalised advice on unit layout and your conversion options: helping you work out which model really is best for you.

- Access to a complete and comprehensive 150-page operations manual which includes

  - Contents lists for your storage boxes and cupboards so you know how to organize for maximum efficiency and can lay your hands to everything you need

- Checklists and routines for typical set up and take down so you forget nothing and trade like a pro from the start

- Step by step guide to frozen dough ball management so you don't end up with wastage

- Tried and tested recipes and detailed ingredients lists so your pizza tastes great from the get go

- Preferred supplier contact details so you know who to trust

- The formulae to identify the profitable events and questions to ask organisers before you book a gig so that you earn money from the start

- What size pizza to offer and whether to box it or not so that you can maximize your profits and charge the maximum for pizza

- Specialisation tricks and tips so that you are always one step ahead of the competition

- Access to prelaunch training days

- Access to a members-only Facebook group

- Access to a monthly Bulletin which keeps you on top of industry trends and includes new recipes, pizza recipes and success insights and tips from leading traders

- Access to a mentoring programme so that if you want it, we can hold your hand and help you grow your business step by step.

To get started on your new journey just call us on +44 1905 621636 or book your discovery seminar online at www.bushmanwoodfiredovens.co.uk.

And don't forget your special bonus!

Get your hands on this free, 11-page, detailed run through of a day in the life of a wedding caterer by visiting http://www.bushmanwoodfiredovens.co.uk/dayinthelife and entering your details.

FULL SPECIFICATION FOR A BUSHMAN WOOD-FIRED OVEN (AND TOOL KIT YOU'LL NEED)

Fully insulated medium Bushman wood-fired oven

This is our most popular oven. It's capable of cooking seventy 10-inch thin and crispy pizzas in an hour. It's available as a standard dome or onion shaped oven.

- Oven dome – with multiple layers of reinforcing and 50mm ceramic high performance insulation complete with reinforced refractory cap
- 4mm high tensile galvanised, multi-strand, straps on turn buckle fasteners
- Oven floor – 4 x pre-cast replaceable high temperature performance cooking tiles
- Oven door – wedge door – with locking latch (for transport)
- Insulated door is an optional extra

For a fully mounted oven that is ready to use, go for our galvanised 300mm deep welded tubular steel frame painted with high heat silver paint, built to support more than the oven's maximum weight. It has:
- Stainless steel capping
- Ceramic under floor insulation (10mm sheet)

Add on a straight chimney kit:
- 7" (900mm) stainless steel twin wall insulated
- 7" flu connector
- 7" insulated flue pipe
- Roof support plate
- Aquarius chimney & flat roof flashing
- Standard cowl
- 2 locking clamps

Or add on the chimney kit for an onion shaped oven:
- Connector 300mm
- Twin wall
- Cover plate
- Aquarius flashing
- Standard cowl

Oven accessories

As a minimum you'll need a pack of three standard basic aluminum peels:
- one 12 inch short handle to keep clean for uncooked pizza
- one 9 inch long handle for rotating and extracting cooked pizza
- one 12 inch long handle for cleaning and feeding the oven

Or you can upgrade to the pro set made with perforated aluminium.
Comes with a 10 cm stainless steel round turning peel and a brass brush.

Thermometer options
- Dial type
- Infra-red
- Built in oven temperature sensor. Shows temperature to 1000°C.

Three possible points – under floor, dome heat and stored oven air

Tool kit
- Fire grate: holds logs off the floor and out of the way. Available in small, medium and large
- Coal hook
- Blow pipe
- Brass brush
- Damp meter (for checking moisture content of wood)
- Gas lighting lance
- Portable weed burner (for fast kindling lighting with minimal smoke)
- Wooden Serving Bat (base for pizza making)
- Hot coal collection snuff box
- Fire extinguisher
- Axe and chopping log; also electric log splitter

CONCLUSION

And there you have it. All you need to consider if you want success in the world of wood-fired catering. So if you are thinking about entering this wonderful world, then I would love to be able to help you on that journey and help you find the financial freedom you personally strive for and the life style you dream of.

I won't say it's easy but if you have passion, drive and determination then why not? This life is yours for the taking.

Give me a call to arrange one of my two hour discovery consultations and let the journey begin!

CONTACT BUSHMAN WOOD-FIRED OVENS

Jay Emery
Kidderminster
Worcestershire
01905 621636

jay@bushmanwoodfiredovens.co.uk
www.bushmanwoodfiredovens.co.uk

Acknowledgements

To my many customers who kindly allowed me to use their testimonials and pictures.

Any business without dedicated staff would not be a good one, so a huge thanks to my support team, John, Simon, Helen and Judith. Thanks guys, I could not do it without you.

Thanks to Tamsen Harward who took my ramblings and turned them into this concise introduction to wood-fired catering. Without her efforts this would have been a jumble of ideas rather than a useful book.

Also thanks to Jane Scott for book design and for pulling it all together so slickly.

And lastly to my parents who taught me from a young age not to be afraid of hard work. To dream big and who encouraged me to be creative and entrepreneurial turning my thoughts into things and things into money.

Disclaimer

This book has been written in good faith and is based on my own experience in the wood-fired oven catering business. You will need to make your own mind up as to which route you take by listening to the advice of your coach builder and verifying that information with your local Food Safety Officer.

On the whole I have found the Food Standards Agency and their Environmental Health Officers to be very helpful and would recommend that you have a proactive relationship with them, rather than relying on them to seek you out.

(Advice on Regulations provided by Worcestershire Regulatory Services)

23995556R00048

Printed in Great Britain
by Amazon